Harold Arthur Fraser, William George Tozer, James Christie

**The East African Slave Trade**

And the Measures Proposed for its Extinction , as Viewed by Residents in Zanzibar

Harold Arthur Fraser, William George Tozer, James Christie

**The East African Slave Trade**
*And the Measures Proposed for its Extinction , as Viewed by Residents in Zanzibar*

ISBN/EAN: 9783743384170

Manufactured in Europe, USA, Canada, Australia, Japa

Cover: Foto ©ninafisch / pixelio.de

Manufactured and distributed by brebook publishing software
(www.brebook.com)

Harold Arthur Fraser, William George Tozer, James Christie

**The East African Slave Trade**

THE

# EAST AFRICAN SLAVE TRADE,

AND THE

MEASURES PROPOSED FOR ITS EXTINCTION,

AS VIEWED BY RESIDENTS IN ZANZIBAR.

BY

## CAPTAIN H. A. FRASER,

## THE RIGHT REV. BISHOP TOZER,

AND

## JAMES CHRISTIE, M.D.

———————

LONDON:

HARRISON, 59, PALL MALL,

BOOKSELLER TO HER MAJESTY AND H.R.H. THE PRINCE OF WALES.

——

1871.

# PREFACE.

I HAVE been requested by my friends in Zanzibar to superintend the publication of the three following papers, written under the force of a strong feeling as to the futility of the measures recommended to the English Government by the Commission on the East African Slave Trade appointed in 1870, and with a further view of enlightening the public generally as to the actual state of things in Zanzibar, especially as to the nature of slavery under Arab masters, and the actual condition of East African slaves. The writers, who are among the oldest and most respected Europeans resident on the east coast, represent three different classes of mind and of experience. Captain Fraser has with indomitable energy devoted himself for a long. time past to the development of the industrial and commercial capabilities of the town and island. No apter representative of commerce could have been found. Dr. Christie, by means of his very extensive medical practice among natives of all classes, has enjoyed rare opportunities, of which he has fully availed himself, of acquiring an insight into the modes of life and current ideas of all ranks from the Sultan to the slave. I can myself confirm a large part of his very complete account of the status and habits of Zanzibar slaves and freed men. Bishop Tozer, while representing the directly missionary

A 2

interest, can tell us better than any one else what strikes a Christian bishop who finds the success of his own work materially affected by the wisdom and humanity either evident or evidently wanting in the proceedings of his own Government.

I am not sure that my friends would be perfectly of one mind as to the details of any plan for the extinction of the East African Slave Trade. Their object was not to propound a plan of their own, but to lay before their countrymen a plain statement of the facts of the case, showing what is the existing state of things, and how very inadequate the means proposed by the Commission were to effect any real improvement.

Since these papers were written a Committee of the House of Commons has been appointed and has made its report upon the subject of the East African Slave Trade. The Committee has in effect recommended nothing except that stronger efforts should be made to put down the Slave Trade, and that the released slaves should be landed at Seychelles, a scheme which has already been tried and found impracticable. Meanwhile the recommendations of the Commission of 1870 have been acted upon.

The measures which ought to be taken to suppress the slave traffic by sea must ultimately be determined upon by our naval authorities; it is, I believe, thought that the best method would be to set a sufficient number of rather small vessels to watch the Arabian coast. When stationed there they would not harass the lawful trade to India, nor that along the African coast, neither could they be baffled by passes to Lamoo, or any other place, like those which are now taken to serve as blinds, when the real destination of the vessel is not Lamoo but some Arabian port, probably Soor or Ras al Kheymah. In any case the Admiralty at home must really try more than it has done hitherto to understand the necessities of the case, to send out full information and wise instructions, and to give praise and blame to the Commanders on the station in a just and discriminating manner. It is very necessary for the vindication of our national honour that dhows should be condemned in some town where the owners have a chance of appearing and of disputing the condemnation. The proceedings of the prize courts in many cases have been nothing more than a one-sided action upon the mere unsifted statement of the captors.

I think all those who have any actual knowledge of East African slavery are agreed that the horrors of the march to the coast, and of the sea passage, can scarcely be exaggerated, but that the moral degradation of both slave and master is the worst feature of actual slavery under Arab owners. Apprentices to an English sugar planter would be in almost every respect worse off than a slave now is. We have not now to deal with anything which at all resembles the old West Indian, or the more recent United States slavery. The English were infinitely worse masters than the Arabs are, and even now Englishmen generally have a very much less kindly feeling towards a free negro than the Arabs have towards their slaves. To apply to the condition of an East African slave the descriptions which were most truthful when applied to one in the West Indies, must provoke something between indignation and amusement in the mind of anyone who knows how the case really stands. If the character of the East African in his own home could be raised, the Slave Trade would cease of itself, and the suppression of the external trade is a help to this end so far as it diminishes the temptation to East Africans to sell their captives and their own children, sets them to work to find or make other articles of export, and so makes society more settled, industry more necessary, and improvement easier.

To put a stop to the horrible cruelties of the slave caravan and the slave ship, is a very worthy object for any Christian nation, but then it must be followed by a real care for those who are released, or else our philanthropy condemns itself. Why do we dislike slavery? The only good reason is because we wish to see all our fellowmen civilized and happy, because, in a word, we love our neighbours as ourselves. To take a man out of a slave dhow and cast him loose to perish in a strange country is no philanthropy. To give to our sailors five pounds a head for every slave they set free, and then grudge the freed slave one night's lodging, or one meal of food, is so absurd that unless one had seen it actually proposed it must have seemed incredible. If the British nation cannot afford to take care of the freed slave, and help him to understand the privileges and duties of a free man, it has no right whatever to take him under its care at all, or to set ships-of-war to take him out of slavery, and leave him a prey to utter ignorance, to disease, and to starvation.

It must be remembered that a freed slave does not merely require protection; he wants a start in life and time and food to make him strong enough to work. He wants, too, government. Captain Fraser mentions a case where the Sultan was in effect fined ten pounds for meddling with a drunken man in the streets of Zanzibar.

It is evident that somebody ought to have punished him, and somebody ought to have power to see that the freed slaves are getting an honest living, and to set them to work for the public benefit if they are not. But the Consul has no time for such things if he had the power.

Every one who can claim to be an authority seems to be agreed that the best measure in regard to the disposal of freed slaves would be to give them a home and a chance of maintaining themselves by the cultivation of the ground in some place on the African coast, where the freed slaves could in time develop into a free negro nation, and over this settlement there must be a special superintendent, responsible for the care of them, and with full power to punish when necessary.*

Any measures short of this can only be in the nature of a makeshift. In any case, however, the British nation must provide temporary food and shelter, a safe protection, and a kindly but firm superintendence for all, for the sick medicine and care, and for the young a home and education. If we will not provide such necessaries as these, our interference with the East African Slave Trade can only serve to cover us with well-merited disgrace.

EDWARD STEERE.

*Little Steeping, October*, 1871.

---

* *Extract from a letter from the Rev. C. Kirk, Chaplain at Aden.*—" It " makes one's blood boil to see how manumitted slaves suffer. Poor things ! " It had almost been better for the grown up ones to go back to the easy " slavery of Arabia. The real want is a settlement on the East Coast, like " Sierra Leone on the West, and to make as much of Bishop Tozer as has " been made of the Bishops of Sierra Leone. That active Bishop would " make a little money go a long way ; we at Aden make much go a little."

THE

# EAST AFRICAN SLAVE TRADE.

## ZANZIBAR AND THE SLAVE TRADE.

BY

CAPTAIN H. A. FRASER, late H.E.I.C.S.

THE Report of the Commission on the East African Slave Trade, addressed to the late Earl of Clarendon in January, 1870, gives a brief account of the existing slave traffic, and recommends the adoption of certain measures by Her Majesty's Government for its gradual suppression, and for the disposal of the slaves captured and liberated by British cruizers.

It explains that the chief export of slaves is from the dominions of the Sultan of Zanzibar, and that the trade in slaves is divided into a legal and illegal traffic.

The legal traffic, as defined by the laws of Zanzibar, being that carried on within certain prescribed limits by Zanzibar subjects; the illegal traffic being that carried on within those limits by other than Zanzibar subjects, and also that carried on beyond those limits by whoever may be engaged therein.

The origin of slavery in East Africa is lost in obscurity; but shortly after the establishment of Arab power on its seaboard we read of the existence of a maritime slave traffic. This of course continued after the Arabs of Oman conquered Zanzibar and its dependencies in the 17th century until 1847, when Said Said, then Imam of Muscat and Ruler of Zanzibar, entered into a treaty with the British Government, by which he agreed to limit the ex-

port of slaves within the tenth degree of south and the
second degree of north latitude, and to co-operate with
the British Government in suppressing all other traffic in
slaves by sea.

Since the death of Said Said some additional restrictions were made by his son, the late Said Majid, who
succeeded his father in the sovereignty of Zanzibar, other-
wise the treaty remains in full force; therefore in virtue
of its provisions, as well as by prescriptive right, the
Government and people of Zanzibar claim the monopoly
they exercise of the traffic in human flesh.

The mode of counducting this traffic the Report describes in ample detail. It records the organization of
armed expeditions to the countries adjoining Lake Nyassa;
the attack on the victims to be enslaved; the depopula-
tion of the country; the horrors of the journey to the
coast; the numbers murdered or left to die on the road;
but it omits all allusion to the still greater atrocities
perpetrated on the miserable survivors of that dreadful
journey by the dealers who purchase them at Kilwa, the
port of export, for shipment to Zanzibar. Thrust into the
crazy vessels in which they are embarked, with barely
room to stand or sit, with a supply of food and water
barely sufficient for sustenance if favoured with a fair
wind; should the contrary happen, the worst horrors of
starvation speedily ensue, and the dead and dying are
alike, without remorse, thrown overboard. Live skeletons
in hundreds may consequently be seen landed at the
Zanzibar Custom-house, from time to time, exciting
neither pity nor comment among the accustomed and
unsympathising spectators.

A foot note to page 4 of the Report states that, " It is
" not unusual to see sick and feeble slaves lying for days
" before the Custom-house at Zanzibar, because the owners
" will not pay the (import) tax until they see whether the
" slaves will live or die."

It might have been added that the Customs authori-

ties, who have for many years farmed the taxes from the
Zanzibar Government, elect to permit the poor wretches
to perish rather than allow them to "pass," without
receiving payment of the amount of duty for which they
are detained; that the authorities in question, who exercise supreme control at the Custom-house, are natives of
the protected State of Cutch, in British India, carrying on
an extensive business as merchants and bankers in Cutch,
Bombay, and Zanzibar; that they enjoy British protection, and are in every respect subject to British law the
same as every British resident in Zanzibar.

From the legal traffic the Report proceeds to describe
how and by whom the illegal traffic is conducted, and
then details the measures that, in the opinion of the Commission, should be adopted: first to reduce, and ultimately
abolish the entire traffic.

" Seeing," they remark, " the misery and loss of life
" which result from the legal traffic alone, and the facilities
" it affords for carrying on the illegal traffic, we think that
"the time has arrived when the Sultan should be pressed
" gradually to diminish the legal export of slaves from the
" mainland, with a view to its ultimate abolition."

At the first glance this appears to be a wise and politic
recommendation, but a very little investigation will show
it is neither.

Reference to the treaty of 1847, already mentioned,
but of which the Commission appears to take no account
(although some at least of the members must have been
well aware of its existence), will show that its obligations on the signatories are as binding as on the day it
was ratified; and until formally released from their share
of those obligations, voluntarily and freely undertaken,
the British Government cannot, without a direct and gross
breach of faith, adopt the Commission's recommendations.

America, Germany, and France have, in common with
ourselves, treaties with the Sultan of Zanzibar, and are
represented by their respective Consuls. How would a

communication from these gentlemen be received by their several Governments, intimating that Great Britain had deliberately repudiated her treaty obligations to the Sultan, and exerted pressure on him to forego treaty rights solemnly secured to him?

In stating that "the time has arrived when the Sultan should be pressed," &c., the Commission assign as a reason that the slave traffic involves much misery and loss of life. Doubtless; but has this fact only come to light in 1870? Was it not equally notorious long prior to the ratification of the treaty of 1847? which secured to the Sultan the continuance of the *legal* slave traffic.

Beyond adverting to the facts, the Commission do not explain why the support accorded by Great Britain to the Sultan, together with the obligation on his part to co-operate in suppressing the *illegal* slave traffic, should form just grounds for compelling him to suppress the *legal* slave traffic, which has been by Treaty secured to him and his subjects: and in the absence of any explanation, the non-diplomatic mind will probably be generally too obtuse to appreciate the force of their reasoning, and the obvious nature of the conclusions deduced therefrom.

Further on, the Commission deprecate the immediate prohibition of the export of slaves, " As such a course, if " adopted, would, whilst reducing the Sultan's revenue, " tend greatly to weaken his power, and by rendering him " unpopular with his subjects; possibly lead to the loss of " his throne, or even his life."

Moreover, they continue, " They fear that the rapidly " increasing commerce of Zanzibar might be ruined if it " were at once deprived of the slave labour on which it " has hitherto relied, before proper provision is made for " supplying free labour in its stead."

Passing over for the present the prior questions, let us inquire what is the value of the commerce of Zanzibar, and what, on the Commission's own showing, the cost at which this commerce is to be maintained.

In round numbers the whole import and export trade of Zanzibar may be grossed at £3,000,000. Taking the Commission's estimate that twenty thousand slaves annually pass through the Kiloa Custom-house, and that these comprise only one-fifth of the number originally dispatched to Kiloa from the interior, we have thus one hundred thousand fellow-creatures dragged into slavery every year, of whom, we are informed, *eighty thousand are murdered or die on the road!*

Making every allowance for a large decrease in the number of slaves which may be expected at Kiloa yearly, after the publication of orders for the gradual suppression of the export traffic, is the maintenance of the commerce of Zanzibar worth so costly a price? I am confident the general response will be that of indignant dissent.

But is the ruin of the commerce of Zanzibar the inevitable sequence of the immediate suppression of the export slave traffic? I, as a Zanzibar merchant of some experience, repudiate the idea, and am assured that all my fellow-countrymen resident in Zanzibar will endorse my opinion.

Present inquiry will, no doubt, ensue, but there need be no apprehension of the ruin anticipated by the Commission. Indeed, I fail to see on what grounds the Commission hazard the assertion, that the commerce of Zanzibar has hitherto relied upon slave labour; and were it worth while, the statement could be easily refuted.

But the recommendations of the Commission involve two postulates which claim further comment.

These are, 1st. That the Sultan has the power to issue and enforce the edicts necessary to accomplish the gradual suppression of the export slave trade. 2nd. That such suppression would ensure the attainment of the ends sought.

To estimate the correct value of the first, it must be understood that the title of Sultan has not the value in the eyes of the Arabs that it possesses for the mass of

Englishmen. To the former it is the designation of a petty chief.

The title was first applied officially by the Indian Government after the death of Said Said, already mentioned, on the division of his possessions into the separate Governments of Muscat and Zanzibar, and their allotment to his two eldest sons.

Both, however, considered the title derogatory, and abstained from its use. The late Sultan of Zanzibar signed himself simply "Majid bin Said," and was invariably addressed by his subjects by prefixing the honorary title of "Seyd" to his name, as is the custom in addressing all Arabs of rank allied to the Sultan by blood. The status occupied by the Sultan of Zanzibar is simply that of a feudal chief elected by the will of the people. As such, he neither possesses the power to make new laws, nor abrogate old ones; and were he to attempt to usurp such power, he would, no doubt, speedily suffer the fate anticipated by the Commission, with probably this difference, that it would be equally the same, whether he attempted the immediate or the gradual suppression of the legal slave traffic.

It is greatly to be feared, however, that under whatever conditions the maritime slave trade of Zanzibar is abolished, whether by force, or by amicable negotiation, involving money payment, as compensation, the majority, if not the whole, of the wealthy Arabs of Zanzibar and Pemba will migrate to the mainland, and establish themselves at "Dar Salaam," which the late Sultan was rapidly making into an important town, in view of such a contingency, at the time of his death.

The influx of a numerous and wealthy body of Arabs, to a country of unsurpassed fertility and unlimited extent, would inevitably create a large demand for slaves, and the venue would simply be shifted from Kilwa to Dar Salaam, which would in future become the nucleus of the slave trade, from whence all the maritime towns to the north, such as Mombas, Lamoo, Brava, could easily obtain their supplies by the land route along the coast.

Nor is it improbable, that on the establishment of such a colony at Dar Salaam, numerous settlers from the disturbed districts of Arabia may arrive to swell the number attracted by the inducements of cheap slaves and a fertile country.

The land traffic will, therefore, not cease to be carried on as heretofore, notwithstanding the entire suppression of the maritime slave trade.

Passing over the less important suggestions and recommendations of the Commission as of minor interest, I come to those referring to the " disposal of the liberated slaves."

These, the Commission recommend, should be landed principally at Zanzibar, "because we understand there is " a great and increasing demand for free labour at that " place, and that even children can readily obtain work at " good wages, so that no charge for their maintenance is " likely to be thrown on the Imperial Government."

I have endeavoured, but in vain, to discover from whence this " great and increasing demand for free labour " arises.

So far as I can ascertain, British subjects alone would hail its introduction as a boon, and a comparatively small number would supply their wants.

The children who at present find work at good wages are, without exception, slaves, owned generally by the poorer class of Arabs, Sawahili, and natives of the Comoro Islands settled in Zanzibar, and are domesticated in their owners' houses, forming integral portions of their families.

Probably such men as well as the large mass of Arab and Sawahili landowners, would readily avail themselves of free labour, as slaves became scarce, but under whatever restrictions liberated slaves might be supplied, it requires no gift of prophecy to foretel, that no long time would elapse before they would be found occupying precisely the same status as the slave population—possibly worse.

The Commission further recommend that liberated slaves in Zanzibar, " should be under the special pro-" tection of Her Majesty's Consul, although amenable to " the laws of Zanzibar."

" They should be provided with printed certificates of " freedom, and as we have already suggested, the Sultan " should declare his intention to punish severely any " attempt to molest them."

It would require very strong pressure indeed, to compel the Sultan to consent to the introduction of hordes of liberated slaves into Zanzibar, increasing in number annually, nominally his subjects, and amenable to the law of the country; but being under British protection, entitled to appeal beyond his jurisdiction to the British Consul, thus establishing an *imperium in imperio*, fatal to, because incompatible with his independence.

The following incident will illustrate the nature of the complications likely to be of too frequent occurrence, consequent on the increase of the Sultan's subjects entitled to British protection.

A few months since a freed slave enjoying this privilege, owing to his being in the employ of a British subject, was apprehended by the night patrol, on the charge of being drunk—placed in the stocks, and next day underwent the penalty always awarded to a negro in such a case, whether bond or free, viz., an unmerciful flogging. A complaint was made to the Acting Political Agent, who promptly demanded satisfaction from the Sultan. It was proved however, that it was not known the man was under British protection, and that he had not mentioned the fact to any one, therefore the payment of £10 to the man by the Sultan, was considered sufficient amends.

The enforcement however of any penalty for flogging

a negro for such an offence would be met with universal indignation by the Arab population, and probably cause serious disturbances.

Up to this point, I have confined my remarks to the Report of the Commission, but I would fain go beyond it, to record my feeble protest against the inhuman and selfish policy that has throughout characterized the national effort to suppress the East African Slave Trade; strong words, but not more so than justice demands.

It is not the mere expenditure of a certain yearly sum, to support a squadron for the repression of the traffic, that will relieve the country from the reproach of acting selfishly, nor will the release of any number of slaves per annum, save it from the stigma of inhumanity.

Contrast the slave located in Zanzibar, with the slave liberated by Great Britain.

Throughout the island, scattered among the cocoa-nut and clove plantations, thousands of huts are to be seen—certainly not built in accordance with European ideas of comfort; but not the less suiting the taste and wants of their occupants: both inside and outside they will in general be found tolerably clean; every hut has its adjoining bit of cultivation from which the family derive their chief support, as well as a surplus to take to sell in town on market days: a few women busy with their household work are generally to be seen about the doors,—some children—but not many—a good supply of poultry—and perhaps a goat or two, tied out to graze hard by. These are the huts of the plantation slaves, who are mostly married.

Slaves though they are, they do not lead a life approaching to what would be deemed one of physical hardship in Britain. They are housed and sheltered, well fed, and not over-wrought, and they have two consecutive days in every week entirely at their own disposal. Moreover, as a rule, they are considerately and kindly treated by their owners.

B

Where shall we find the freed slave under the protection of Great Britain, living in equal comfort? Where find his cheerful little homestead, brightened by ties dear alike to bond and free? Where shall we look for any such evidence that he is well cared for and contented?

Alas! we may search in vain: the prison islets of Aden, the stews of Bombay, the plantations of Mauritius and Seychelles, tell alike the same disgraceful tale!

There is *no* future provided for the "protected" freed slave, unless one infinitely more hopeless and brutalized, than the lot from which he was forcibly torn.

Is it for this so much treasure is lavished, so much innocent blood shed?

Painful as the question is, how appalling is the answer? The fact is so! Year after year our men-of-war, engaged in the repression of the East African slave trade, have driven numberless native slave vessels ashore in the attempt to effect their capture, causing the death of hundreds, nay, thousands of slaves.

Does this statement require proof? Here is one of many, taken from the Blue Book on the Slave Trade, Class A, from January 1st to December 31st, 1866.

From Lieutenant Commander Garforth to the Secretary to the Admiralty.

"'*Penguin,' Ras Mabber, April* 29, 1866.
" (Extracts.)

"I ceased firing for the sake of the slaves. The "dhow was run on the rocks through a heavy surf to "avoid capture. . . . The dhow filling with water "numbers of slaves were drowned. . . The dhow was "from Zanzibar, bound to Muscat, with over 200 slaves "on board. . . . On the following day she was "totally destroyed. The number of slaves recovered "28."

In a report by the same officer, dated June 20th, 1866,

he states, "Those (masters of dhows) carrying slaves, " will, if possible run their vessels on the rocks, with " almost certain destruction to their vessels and those on " board, sooner than fall into the hands of a white man." And in corroboration of this statement, the Blue Book from which I quote, shows that, during the year, seven dhows were run ashore to escape capture.

Surely such facts staring the Government in the face, should give cause for grave consideration, as to whether a system should be longer suffered to exist, that appears to involve waste of public money, wholesale destruction of life, and shameful neglect of the captured slaves, whom we profess to liberate and protect; without apparently securing any beneficial results whatever, as a set off against these evils.

Nothing, in the Report of the Commission on the East African Slave Trade, appears to indicate that they have given any attention to this subject, as no reference is made to the fact, nor any recommendation of improvement for the future.

No doubt the conscientious adjustment of these and many other important questions relating to the slave trade, and its suppression, present in themselves sufficiently difficult problems for solution. But any just and equitable solution becomes impracticable, which has for its basis only mistaken expediency and false economy.

The interests of humanity, and the national honour of Great Britain are alike involved in the adjustment of these questions, which can neither be evaded nor ignored, and in dealing with them the Government must face their responsibilities boldly, and perform their self-imposed duties honourably and faithfully.

H. A. FRASER.

*Zanzibar, June 1st, 1871.*

# ON THE TREATMENT OF FREED' SLAVES,

BY

## THE RIGHT REVEREND W. G. TOZER, D.D.,

MISSIONARY BISHOP IN CENTRAL AFRICA.

AT the beginning of last year (1870) a Commission which had been appointed by the Foreign Office to consider the whole question of the East African Slave Trade submitted its Report to the late Lord Clarendon. The Report was signed by Mr. Churchill, the then Political Resident and Consul at Zanzibar, Captain Fairfax, who had served on the East Coast some years previously as a Lieutenant on board H.M.S. "Ariel," and five others.

The subsequent accession of Seyid Barghash, the late Sultan's brother, will probably necessitate a re-consideration of the whole question. The present time, therefore, seems favourable for directing attention to the treatment of such slaves as are liberated by our cruizers, and to the suggestions offered by Mr. Churchill and his colleagues under the Commission, for their disposal in future.

Hitherto our men-of-war have landed their prize cargoes of slaves either at Aden, Bombay, Mauritius, or Seychelles. Aden seems to have received a larger number of freed slaves than either of the other depôts, but at none of them are there any satisfactory arrangements for the proper care of these people.

I find, on inquiry, that out of 2,297 slaves landed at Aden between January, 1865, and January, 1869, the " casualties " amounted to no less than 1,046.*

* Lieutenant Colonel Playfair, formerly Assistant Political Resident at Aden, writes privately to me as follows : " The proportion of mortality you give as having occurred amongst the freed slaves at Aden and Bombay is frightful. but my own experience entirely confirms it. I used to find that those landed at Aden were decimated within the year, all from the same cause —disease of the lungs."

To the question—" Does any Government organization
" exist for the education of the children, or for the spiritual
" care of the Negro population?" the answer is in the
negative.

When asked " Do any considerable number profess the
" Mahommedan religion?" my correspondent writes, " The
" bulk do, to get wives, even if servants of Europeans."

At Bombay during five years 1,158 slaves are reported
to have been liberated, in addition I presume to 1,267
received from Aden. The death-rate here is also excep-
tionally high. The Bombay Government, much to its
credit, has maintained 125 children at an industrial school
belonging to the Church Missionary Society; but the
Principal of the Institution has recorded his opinion that
India is no suitable place for Africans. "I do not know,"
he says, in his Report to the Society, " whom I shall
" bewail most, those who after their arrival here are made
" over to Mahommedans, and adopt their religion, or those
" who after having been instructed in the way of life in
" our Institution at Sharanpur, are then thrown amongst
" the very dregs of European society on the railways,
" participate in their sins, and are a shame and dishonour
" to Christianity."

In confirmation of this, the registers of births and
deaths at Bombay show that while in five years the births
did not exceed 37, the deaths among the Negro population amounted to 754.

In Mauritius the younger slave children, as at Bombay,
are lodged and taught in an orphanage at the expense of
the Government, but I understand from one who has
spent some time in the island, that the social and moral
condition of the released slaves is very deplorable; and I
regret to be compelled to say the same of such as I have
myself seen in the Seychelles Islands.

These facts demonstrate with sufficient clearness the
inconsistency of our policy in repressing the East Coast
Slave Trade; for while we maintain a costly squadron

for the capture of slave dhows, and use every exertion to make its operations as effective as possible, we are doing little or nothing for such slaves as fall into our hands. We land them at ports where no adequate provision is made for their reception, either at the time of their liberation or subsequently, where the climate proves fatal in a large number of cases, and where they are regarded by the local authorities as a burden from which they have asked again and again to be relieved.

The Report already referred to devotes the paragraphs numbered from .61 to 71 inclusive, to the "Disposal of " liberated Slaves."

The difficulty of finding suitable employment for Negroes at Aden or Seychelles is admitted, and the Commission recommend Zanzibar as the best depôt for all, or nearly all, the slaves that may be set free from our men-of-war.

The Commission very properly say, " The greatest care " should be taken to provide efficient protection for the " freed slaves, and to prevent their being ill used by their " employers, or kidnapped by slave-dealers;" and they advise that " they," the released slaves, " should be under " the special protection of Her Majesty's Consul, although " amenable to the laws of Zanzibar. A register should be " kept of them at the British Consulate; they should be " provided with printed certificates of freedom; and the " Sultan should declare his intention to punish severely " any attempt to molest them."

Thus four guarantees are offered for the " efficient pro-" tection ". of such slaves as may be liberated at Zanzibar, and I will proceed to examine them separately.

1stly. " *The freed slaves are to be under the special pro-*" *tection of Her Majesty's Consul, although amenable to the* " *laws of Zanzibar."*

These terms I imagine do not describe a position

recognized by existing treaties, but are rather suggested as the basis of a new political status, to meet the case of these liberated slaves. If this be so, I think the Commission should have minutely described this new compact, because the success of their whole scheme depends on the satisfactory adjustment of the existing laws of Zanzibar, with what the Report calls " the special protection of Her " Majesty's Consul."

There are at Zanzibar Banyans and other subjects of certain Indian dependencies who live under the protection of our flag, and claim to be independent of the Sultan's jurisdiction; but I believe that no competent tribunal has defined the exact legal status of these persons. (*See Note A.*)

I have myself received at various times from the British Consulate slave children that have been liberated by English men-of-war, but successive political residents have held the most opposite opinions of their legal position, and no one seems to know precisely whether they are British subjects or under British protection, or, again, subjects of the Sultan of Zanzibar, and amenable to his laws.

If, therefore, large numbers of negroes are to be landed here, as the Commission advise, these many international questions must be fully considered, or the result will be endless complications of every possible kind.

I offer no opinion as to whether an island like Zanzibar is able to maintain continual accessions of freed slaves, but it would appear a contradiction, in terms, to treat these people as subjects of the Sultan, and amenable to his laws, and yet to claim for them some special political privilege, in which the rest of his Highness's subjects had no share.

2ndly. The Commission's next proposal for the efficient protection of the freed slaves is, that " *a register* " *should be kept of them at the British Consulate.*"

But here a difficulty arises at once, for in a large

majority of cases, there will be nothing more distinctive
to register than the slave's sex and height; all else per-
taining to his separate individuality will have been lost,
his very name will have changed whenever he chanced to
pass from one master to another. Under these circumstances the registration of a cargo of slaves would be
very similar to the registration of an equal number of
sheep or cattle; and as a means of future identification
entirely worthless.

3rdly. The next suggestion is, that " *They*," the
slaves, " *should be provided with printed certificates of free-*
" *dom.*"

It appears to me, that such a proposal as this merits a
very severe reproof.

Printed certificates of any kind pre-suppose a certain
advance in the ways of civilised life, but the victims of the
Slave Trade are, as the Commission well knew, poor,
frightened, houseless, and homeless creatures, that arrive
at Zanzibar in a state of the most absolute degradation
and misery.

If the Commission imagined that their expedient of
printed certificates can be of the least possible service to
people in this condition, or that they will shield them in
any degree from the evil designs of the slave dealers and
kidnappers, or protect them from molestation and ill usage,
I can only say that they are labouring under a most fatal
delusion.

4thly. The last guarantee which the Commission pro-
vides for the efficient protection of the liberated slaves is
worded as follows :—

" *The Sultan should declare his intention to punish severely*
" *any attempts to molest them.*"

The Commission have evidently much faith in the
effect of the Sultan's official proclamations, as may be seen
by a reference to other passages in their report; but a

residence of some years in Zanzibar enables me to state—
1st, That the Sultan's proclamations do not invariably
command respect, even when intended to promote the
security and good government of his own Arab subjects;
and 2ndly, That the Zanzibar administration of justice is
such that a few days' seclusion in the fort is recognised as
a suitable punishment even for very serious misde-
meanours; indeed, it is not too much to say that it would
be wholly out of the Sultan's power to " punish severely "
an Arab of standing and position who might be found
" molesting " a liberated slave.

The 66th paragraph of the Report recommends the
deportation of a limited number of the released slaves by
way of experiment to—1st, The French plantations of
Reunion; 2nd, The Island of Johanna; and 3rd, The
Coast of Africa.

It will be remembered that Reunion was for some
years deeply compromised in the eyes of Englishmen by
the employment of negroes under the specious title of
" engagés," and it is due, I believe, to the repeated pro-
tests of our Government, that this system is being suppressed.

At Johanna, which I visited some few years since,
Arab interests are uncontrolled by any English or other
consular agent; indeed, there is but one European resident
in the island.

I and my clergy have frequent occasion to visit the
African Coast, and I feel no hesitation in saying, that the
selection of it, as a possible home for released slaves, must
have been made haphazard, and in ignorance of the daily
risks to which every black man, slave or free, is exposed
who happens to live there.

Before making ventures like these, on the strength of
the political influence, which we may be thought to possess
as a nation, it cannot be stated too plainly, that even now
we are unable to secure " efficient protection " for the few

negro children who are domesticated among us; nor is the English Consulate powerful enough to check and punish such flagrant acts of brutality as too often attend the arrival in harbour of slave dhows from Kiloa. (See Note B).

The plan of repressing the Slave Trade by capturing slaves involves some of the gravest responsibilities imaginable. I offer no opinion of my own as to whether our policy in this respect be right or wrong, but I maintain that we are bound by every principle of honour to do the best we can for the slaves whom we separate from their Arab masters on the plea of humanity.

I have looked in vain for any admission of this kind in the Report; the idea of raising these people in the social scale or making them or their children the agents for raising others, is entirely ignored.

I can only say in conclusion, that if the Commission's scheme should ever be acted upon, it may be true that the slaves landed year by year at Zanzibar, will be free in some subtle political sense of the word, but for all practical purposes, they will be slaves still; and it is because a great nation like England cannot escape her responsibility to these people by simply shunting them out of sight at the least possible cost and trouble, and because such a policy is both short-sighted and delusive, that I feel compelled as a Christian Missionary, to enter my protest against it.

WILLIAM GEORGE TOZER,

*Missionary Bishop.*

*Shangani House,*
  *Zanzibar, June* 7, 1871.

## NOTE A.

A gentleman long resident in Zanzibar has kindly supplied me with the following statement on the matter under discussion :—

" The Indian population resident in Zanzibar is com-
" posed chiefly of natives of the protected State of Cutch,
" comprising Mahommedans of the Koja and Bohora sects,
" and Hindoos principally of the Bhattia caste. These
" have been specially placed under the protection and
" jurisdiction of the British Government, by their
" Sovereign the Rao of Cutch. Prior to this proclamation
" being issued, many of these people had placed them-
" selves under the Sultan's protection, and in virtue
" thereof claimed the right to buy and sell slaves. They
" are, however, though claiming the Sultan's protection,
" amenable to British law, unless they formally de-
" naturalize themselves, and become *bonâ fide* Zanzibar
" subjects; and in cases of slave-dealing they are dealt
" with as any British subject would be."

## NOTE B.

Almost while I write the acting Political Resident has been obliged to send a boy out of the island for whom he had provided an asylum at the Consulate itself.

Systematic attempts to entice him away had been repeatedly successful, and it was thought unsafe for the boy to be any longer exposed to such temptations.

Another case was that of a small child I received from Her Majesty's ship " Star," who strayed out one evening into the town by himself. I communicated immediately with the Consulate, and considerable exertions were made for his recovery, all the officials being most anxious to help me; but though we offered a reward, and had persons watching in every quarter of the town for some days, nothing whatever was heard of the boy again.

The following extract is taken from the *Lancet*, of February 11th :—

" In connection with the epidemic cholera, in May and " June, when the disease was continued in the harbour " by the cholera being returned from the slave mart at " Kiloa, I cannot but mention the shocking condition of " the slaves imported to Zanzibar at that time, although " this is somewhat apart from the subject under consider- " ation. I speak of nothing in connection with this subject " of which I was not an eye-witness, and which I did not " note at the moment.

" During the first two weeks in May several cargoes of " slaves were landed at the Custom-house, in the most " horrible condition imaginable, and I believe that it is " only at the harbour of Zanzibar that a living skeleton, " reduced to that state by compulsory starvation, can be " seen. On May 17th a cargo of slaves in this condition " was landed at the Custom-house. I was informed, and " I have every reason to believe, correctly, that about 250 " had been put on board at Kiloa, with only a little food " and water, in a very small dhow. I saw the dhow " coming into the harbour, with its living cargo crouched " together as closely as people could stand, or could be " packed.

" The dhow had been three days on the passage, and " cholera was said to have broken out on board, 70 having " died. The duty on slaves is paid on their passing " through the Custom-house at Zanzibar, so that, to save " that expense, the dying wretches were left to expire on " the sands, and the living skeletons were driven and " dragged and kicked along past my door during the fore- " noon, and a scene such as this excited no surprise.

" In the evening of the same day, one of the cargo, a " female, was picked up by two other gentleman and " myself at the outskirts of the town, while staggering " towards it, falling down in a state of utter exhaustion " every short time. She was kindly cared for till her death,

" nearly two weeks after, by the Right Rev. Bishop Tozer,
" and her story was to the effect that when the dhow was
" skirting the beach, before coming into the harbour, she
" and two others were thrown overboard, and that the
" water, being shallow, she managed to wade to the shore
" without being drowned, but she thought that the others
" were dead. Such cases are not exceptions, but the rule,
" in the conveyance of slaves. While the woman was alive
" the case was reported to the English Consulate, the
" circumstances stated, and the brand to identify the slave
" was given, but nothing whatever was done by the
" Government of His Highness the Sultan to investigate
" the case and disprove the woman's statement, although
" the case could have been traced with the greatest ease.

" Slaves after landing are, as a general rule, not
" unkindly treated in Zanzibar, but that such scenes as
" occur in slave-dhows during the course of their trans-
" mission should be allowed is a disgrace to civilisation.

" The horrible sufferings to which these miserable
" wretches are wantonly exposed is unsurpassed, indeed,
" it could not be surpassed; and this takes place, as a
" matter of course, in open daylight, without even an
" attempt to screen it, and with the sanction of a Govern-
" ment having treaties with European nations, and, in fact,
" supported by them. Slave gangs are driven through
" the streets in broad daylight, reduced to a skeleton state
" by starvation and disease, men, women, and children,
" none having more than a small piece of coarse bagging
" or some twisted leaves to cover their nakedness, and
" many as naked as when they were born: not children,
" but grown up men and women. No estimate could be
" given of the ravages of the epidemic amongst these, tho
" most miserable of all God's creatures since man was
" created."

These startling revelations are confirmed by the
following statement with which my chaplain, the Rev. R.
L. Pennell, has been kind enough to supply me. The

matter occurred while I myself was absent from Zanzibar :—

" One morning early in June, 1870, as a dhow was
" passing in front of the Mission-house, full of slaves, a
" body was thrown into the water. The action of the
" arms and hands, which several of us witnessed, clearly
" proved that it was not a corpse. I at once went to the
" Political Resident, and informed him of the circumstance.
" The owner and captain of the dhow were immediately
" summoned, but as they strenuously denied the fact, no
" further proceedings were taken, nor were those members
" of the mission, who had witnessed the outrage, asked
" for their evidence.

"W. G. T."

# SLAVERY IN ZANZIBAR AS IT IS.

BY

## JAMES CHRISTIE, M.D., M.A.

1. Condition of Slaves employed on the Farms or Plantations.
2. Condition of Slaves employed in the Town.
3. Laws and Customs in regard to Slaves.
4. Condition of Freeborn and Freed Negroes.
5. Recommendations of the Commission.
6. The Slave Trade in the Interior, and its cure.

---

1. *Condition of Slaves employed on the Farms or Plantations.*

The estates of the Arabs are not leased, but worked at the expense and risk of the individual proprietors. Many of these estates are in different parts of the island and on the mainland, although possessed by one individual. To carry on the work of these estates a wealthy Arab may have one thousand or more slaves. The proprietor personally, or through his agents, disposes of the produce, and the estates are left in charge of Arabs, who may have no independent means, or under the supervision of trustworthy freed slaves. Many Arab proprietors reside in the town of Zanzibar and take no active part in the management of their estates, some, however, reside upon them, and only come to town to dispose of their produce.

In carrying on the work of an estate there are three head-men; the Msimamizi, who is generally free; the Nokoa, who is the head-slave; and the Kadamu, the second head slave, the two last being invariably slaves. There are also other slaves who have minor charges in carrying on particular work, and those in charge are generally selected from the Wazalia, *i.e.*, those born on the estate, or from those, among the directly imported slaves, who display superior intelligence. Practically, the carrying on of the work is under the supervision of those selected from among the slaves themselves, the master, or his deputies, interfering but little in regard to the actual work done.

According to the computation of Arabs who own estates the profit derived from their slaves does not amount to five dollars, or one pound annually per head, and in the majority of cases they state that it is much less than the half of this.

The average price of a slave for country work is at present from twenty-five to thirty dollars, being nearly double the price of the same class of slaves a few years ago. But even this is a very low sum as compared with the price of slaves in other parts of the world. It seems strange or even incomprehensible that the sum paid for possession of a man should be about half of that paid for a very ordinary donkey, but such is the case. This apparent anomaly may be understood when the position of the slave in Zanzibar is considered, for except in the fact of their being slaves, the Zanzibar slaves and those formerly held by Europeans are different in almost every respect.

The newly imported slaves purchased by the Arabs for work on their estates are generally in a very reduced bodily condition, more especially those who are brought from the Nyassa district, and are unfit for any kind of work for months. They are supported on the estate until such time as they may be able to enter upon active employment, and in the meantime they receive their allotment of land for cultivation on their own account, which, as they are able, they clear and plant.

Every slave on an estate, has his hut and patch of land, called " Koonde," sufficient in extent for the support of himself and family. The huts are scattered in small clusters and have a very neat comfortable appearance, and the Koonde are generally in a good state of cultivation.

They are not all of a uniform size, for if a slave is industrious and has sufficient time at his disposal he may cultivate, on his own account, as much land as he pleases, within reasonable limits. From this he must support and clothe himself, and the proceeds of the surplus crop are entirely at his own disposal. The more industrious plant considerably in excess of what is required for their necessary wants, and they also possess goats and fowls for which they can always find a ready market. The slaves are encouraged by their masters in such respects, as they regard habits of industry and the possession of property as evidence of attachment to the estate, the slave having a personal interest in it. The master has, in addition, a certain guarantee for the honesty and good conduct of the slaves, for, although the produce belongs absolutely to the slave, the master has something that he can seize in case of default. The property of a slave is sacred, and no master, however powerful, would dare to deprive him of it unless in cases of delinquency.

The slaves are encouraged to contract marriages and live in family, and in the event of their not finding wives on the estate it is customary to purchase those for them to whom they have formed an attachment. The marriages are regarded as binding in the same sense as they are amongst the Arabs, but they are not contracted before the Kathi, the master of the estate or his deputy being in the place of and having the same power as the Kathi. The offspring of these marriages are called " Wazalia," and they occupy a much higher position among the slave population than those who have been brought directly from the mainland.

The slaves on the estates are supported and clothed by their masters only until such time as their allotment

C

produces its crop, and after that time no further payment or allowance is made on account of the slaves, except in special cases. The slaves are at the disposal of the master for five days in the week, the two remaining days, Thursday and Friday, belonging to themselves. On these days they cultivate their own patches of land, and in the crop season convey the produce to town for disposal. At daybreak the drum is beaten at the house of the Msimamizi, and the slaves muster for work, which may continue till about four o'clock, but it is rarely that any field work is done after twelve. During the clearing, planting, and crop season the whole strength of the estate is called into requisition, and while the clove crop is being secured, it being necessary to proceed as rapidly as possible to prevent loss, the slaves often work for seven days in the week, but this is always a matter of arrangement, and they are recompensed for their extra services. This is readily arranged between master and slave as the latter has at his own disposal, at less busy times, a considerable portion of the five days during which his master is entitled to his services. The value of an estate in Zanzibar depends principally on the number of the bearing cocoa-nut and clove trees. The cocoa-nut crop is continuous throughout the year, but the clove crop must be gathered and cured within a definite period, and the proprietor must have sufficient hands to accomplish this, as labour beyond the estate cannot at that time be procured. A large number of slaves is therefore necessary, and the proprietor can afford the outlay of the purchase-money for the slaves, allowing them to support themselves by the cultivation of intermediate crops on their own account. No Arab estate is cultivated to its full capability, and there does not seem to be any desire on the part of the proprietors that it should be so. Were this attempted it would be necessary to pay the slaves, and to exact from them much more work than by the present system.

Thus, hard work is ignored by both master and slave,

and one may ride over the most populous and best cultivated parts of the island for miles during the day without
seeing anyone engaged in field work, except on the slavo's
own allotments.  Strangers are invariably surprised at the
deserted appearance of the fields, which form a striking
contrast to the description of slave plantations in other
countries.  The hardest work which the slaves have to
undergo consists in carrying on their heads the produce of
the estates to the town of Zanzibar or to the harbours
contiguous to the estates, there being no roads on the
island suitable for cartage.

Many of the wealthy Arabs who possess estates are
largely engaged in business, and they organize and send
to central Africa large and valuable caravans for the sale
of goods and purchase of ivory and slaves.  A trading
expedition of this kind would not be considered very large
if composed of five hundred men or from that to one
thousand, so that such ventures are of considerable value,
and they are very often shared in by Indo-British subjects.

These caravans are generally accompanied by several
Arabs who have a small interest in the concern, but the
success of the expedition is entirely dependent on the
freed men or slaves to whom are entrusted property
of great value.  Men of this class are generally selected
from among the Wazalia, i.e., those born on the estate,
and a position of this kind is one of the highest to which
a slave aspires.  When he has thus proved himself to be a
person of intelligence and trust, he is generally freed,
assumes the Arab dress, and associates with his former
master on the footing of an Arab of inferior family.  He
generally remains in the service of his former master, and
is devotedly attached to his interests, the relationship
between the two being almost identical with that of patron
and client.

As a matter of course it occasionally happens, from
some misfortune, that a person of wealth is reduced to a
state of poverty, and in such cases his freed slaves con-

sider themselves bound to support him.  Cases are not uncommon in which slaves thus freed and who have become
rich men, support and regard themselves as responsible
for the bringing up of their late master's family, and
it-is but rarely that such obligations are disregarded.

Every one acquainted with the subject must admit that
the slaves of this class are well treated by their masters,
that harsh measures are seldom resorted to, and that when
punishments are inflicted they are so judicially.

These remarks are not made in palliation of slavery,
but as statements of facts to be referred to hereafter.

### 2. *Condition of Slaves employed in the Town.*

These may be divided into different sections, as
follows—domestic slaves, ordinary unskilled labourers,
porters, skilled labourers, and artisans.

In every Arab household there is a large number of
domestic slaves, out of all proportion to the amount of
work done.  It is considered to be a mark of dignity and
importance to have a crowd of household slaves, and the
number indicates the wealth and dignity of the master.
They are generally selected from amongst those born on
the estate, and amongst them there are several grades.
The domestic servants of the natives of India and of
Europeans are nearly all slaves, and their number may be
estimated at about one thousand.  The natives of India
pay about a dollar a month and supply food and clothing.
In cases of severe illness the slaves are transferred to the
house of the master, to whom all the money payment
goes.  Those thus employed are women and children.
The wages of the servants of Europeans are from two and
a half dollars per month and upwards.  They are supposed
to find themselves in provisions, but as a matter of fact
they do not.  The wages are paid to the servants, and the
proportion given to the owner is a matter of arrangement
between slave and master.

The ordinary day labourers are employed in a great

variety of occupations. They are of both sexes and average from seven or eight years, upwards, their daily wages being from eight to twenty pice per day. Children from seven or eight years can always earn eight pice (threepence three farthings) daily. Boys from ten and twelve can earn ten pice, and if experienced twelve pice, a little more than five pence. Youths and adults can earn from fourteen to twenty pice, or ninepence three farthings.

The estimated expenditure for the support of the children at the Universities' Mission at Zanzibar is six pounds annually, or fourpence per day, a little more than eight pice, the lowest rate of wages paid to children; this includes every item of expenditure except rent and supervision. Their food and clothing is much superior to that of the ordinary native population, who can live on three pice daily for provisions.

The scale of wages paid by the Indo-British subjects is rather lower than this, the European scale; and although the sum may appear small, it is much higher than the rate of wages in Europe for unskilled labour, when the small expenditure for the necessaries of life is taken into account. The hours of labour are from six o'clock in the morning till five in the afternoon, with an hour and a half, and often two hours, for dinner. It would be difficult to form an estimate of the number of this class of slaves, but it cannot be under from ten to fifteen thousand daily. Employment can always be had, and there is no necessity for any one being idle. Indeed the demand for labour exceeds the supply. Children are employed in the picking of orchilla weed; youths and adults in the cleaning of gum copal, breaking cocoa-nuts, and preparing the copra, carrying small loads, loading and discharging cargoes, and numerous other branches of industry.

The domestic life of this section of the slave population is entirely different from that of the class first alluded to, viz., the slaves employed on the farms or plantations.

They are owned for the most part by the poorer class of Arabs, who do not possess estates, by the settlers from Johanna and Comoro, and by slaves. The object of the wealthy Arabs possessing estates is to have a sufficient number of people on their farms to secure and convey their crops to market, and being indifferent regarding soil cultivation, they recompense them by giving them land for cultivation on their own account; but the object of the owners of the town slaves is primarily to procure the means of existence.

The day labourers work much harder and more constantly than the country labourers are obliged to do, and the arrangements for their support are very different.

They make their appearance early in the morning at the various houses where labour is regularly required, or at the custom-house, and in the evening they receive their pay. No arrangements are made with the owners of the slaves, and no money payments are made to them by the employers of labour. Indeed, in so far as they are concerned, they know nothing about the people employed, whether they are slaves or free. Those who do the work receive from them the pay, and as to the disposal thereof, that is a matter of arrangement between owner and slave.

In regard to these arrangements, there is no invariable rule; but the lowest allowance made is one pice on going out in the morning, a full meal on returning in the evening, what little clothing they require, and house accommodation. Such cases are exceptional, and would not be tolerated by the slaves for any length of time. It is more common to allow them two or three pice. In the case of children and youths this is generally done, but in regard to adults it is very common to receive from the slaves at the rate of eight pice daily, the surplus earnings being their own.

It is difficult to understand how any one can procure a meal by the purchase of one or two pice worth of provisions, but this is done by six or more laying out their pice in the purchase of different articles, and then sharing the common supply. Every master knows perfectly well that if his slaves are not well fed and comfortable, according to their own ideas, they cannot or would not work, and that, unless able for work, they would not get employment in any of the mercantile houses. There is thus a certain guarantee for the receipt of the necessaries of life. The slaves live along with their masters, and the master is in regard to them *in loco parentis*. While at work there are no cruel measures used to force excessive labour, and their work is superintended by those of their own class. The employers of labour are well aware that if harsh measures were resorted to, they would be unable to carry on their work, for the whole gang would at once clear out. It has frequently happened that on a slave being struck on board ship, the whole of those employed have gone over the ship's side and swam on shore refusing to resume work again; and when this occurs, it is extremely difficult to supply their place by a new gang. If a slave is maltreated, he complains to his master, who at once appears in his interest, and the same takes place if he has been accidentally injured.

It is not to be supposed that the master does this from any high philanthropic sentiments. He does it simply because he and his slaves have common interests, and if one suffers the other must suffer also. The slaves work and the masters look after the interests of their slaves, and afford them protection. The necessity for this protection will be referred to hereafter.

The next class of labourers are the porters or hamalis. There being no cartage in Zanzibar, all the heavy burdens connected with the loading and discharging of ships and the transfer of goods from one part of the town to another, are carried on men's shoulders by means of poles. These men are nearly all imported slaves and they go through a great amount of heavy work.

They are all powerful men and are selected by their owners for this particular kind of work. It is difficult to understand how these men can be got to bear such heavy burdens all day long. A few years ago it was common for Arabs from Hadramaut to work as porters along with the slaves, and then it was considered necessary to employ such free labour in order to induce the negroes to go through their heavy tasks.

At present Arabs are rarely employed in such work, and only when compelled to it by necessity. The masters of these slaves are nearly all Arabs from Hadramaut. All the porterage is done by contract or according to a scale of charges on articles conveyed. The parties making these arrangements do not own all the slaves employed, but make agreements with those possessing a few slaves for their work. The Zanzibar merchants and others requiring such work do not pay the workers directly but their masters, so that in regard to recompense the matter is entirely between the contractor or the masters and porters. The master is responsible for theft and destruction of property, and claims of this kind, which are of frequent occurrence, are generally met with but little trouble. Merchants would with great difficulty carry on their business without parties who were responsible for the transit of their goods, for the negro will steal if he can get the chance. These men work under the immediate superintendence of Arabs, and they resent all interference in regard to the mode of performing their work or any attempt at punishment in case of default, except at the hands or by the orders of those in charge of them. They form a very distinct class, and look upon themselves as superior to the country slaves and ordinary day labourers, and they consider it a degradation to carry anything which does not require the poles.

When not required by their masters for contract labour the proceeds of any work done by them are their own, and when they work overtime, which is often the case, extra payments made belong to themselves. They are much better fed and provided for than the former class of slaves. Some live in the houses of their masters, but many in huts of their own.

The next and last class of slaves to be considered is the artisan class, if they can be so called.

They represent, but in a very rough form, the artisan class of civilised countries. They are nearly all slaves and slave owners, and their arrangements with their masters are very various. A carpenter or mason can earn from a quarter to half a dollar daily, but he is by no means willing to hand over the whole of this sum to his master, merely accepting the necessaries of life in return. The master has a special claim on his slave when he himself requires work done, but an arrangement is made between them as to what proportion of his earnings from others the master is to receive, and such agreements when once entered into are rarely broken. In all such cases the slave is the more independent of the two, for if the master is exacting and presses hard upon the slave, refusing to allow more than the means of subsistence, the latter can refuse to work longer as a skilled labourer and place himself in the position of an ordinary day labourer. The master is thus entirely in the hands of his slaves. It is but rarely that there is any necessity for such a stand being made, but cases of this kind do occasionally occur. Those of this class act very independently with their owners, and in regard to trade combinations they present a bolder front, with a much simpler organisation, than the trade unions of Great Britain.

When working for Europeans their charges are higher than when working for others, and although the rate of pay may rise it does not fall. During the last few years the wages have risen considerably. They never work more than eight hours, and during that time they do less than an European workman would do in half the time. If a workman, say a mason, has been regularly employed, either constantly or at intervals, as a head man, and, if he is discharged for some fault, the whole of those working with or under him stop work, and refuse to resume it until he is restored to his former position. They ignore the question of culpability, and it is usually in vain to search for others to supply their places. They say, "This is your man, and you must take him and the whole gang back to your employment." Cases frequently occur, in which this stand is made by workmen, and they generally, if not invariably, succeed in their demand. There is no difficulty in maintaining such a position, for although they strike work they can procure immediate employment as unskilled labourers, and earn sufficient to meet their wants. In a tropical country the wants of the people are comparatively few, and the necessaries of life abundant. In Zanzibar no one need die of starvation, and appearances of poverty and distress do not present themselves in the horrible forms that meet one's eye in European countries. Poverty, in fact, does not exist, and the beggars are so professionally.

Although the mass of the slave population is employed as has been described, great numbers are engaged in various occupations, such as the navigation of coasting craft and as sailors in native dhows; in fishing, cutting firewood, &c. The slaves employed on the estates live more in family than those in town, and their social and moral condition is superior. To a certain extent they adopt the religion and manners of their masters, and the Wazalia always do so and are strictly Mahometan. Drunkenness is not a prevalent vice, and it is but very rarely that a slave is seen in a state of intoxication. To be intoxicated is a crime according to the Zanzibar laws, and the person is liable to imprisonment and flogging. Petty thefts are very common, and it is next to impossible to rely on the honesty of any one. Housebreaking is not of very frequent occurrence, and violence to the person is very rare, much more so than in civilized countries. One may reside for years in the island, and pass through any part of the town at all times without molestation. Considering that every native is armed, although it be but with a knife, it is surprising that so few murders do occur. In the island the number of slaves in proportion to their masters must be at least fifty to one, and the masters, knowing the latent power they have to control, manage their slaves with great prudence and tact, and never have the least fear of a servile revolt.

The slave knows very well that there are certain orders that he must obey, and that he must do a certain amount of work for his master, but he knows equally well that the masters dare not and would not transgress the understood privileges and acknowledged rights of their slaves.

The slave looks to his master for protection, and regards him as his natural guardian, bound to exert all his influence in his behalf if injured. He also looks to him for support when unable to work through sickness.

The name slave is not in itself considered to be a term of reproach. It is the common term for a servant, whatever his rank may be, and is only applied in a contemptuous manner in connection with the name of a master of no position.

The domestic and country slaves of powerful Arab chiefs regard themselves as persons of no ordinary importance, and amongst the coloured population, both free and bond, the *status* is fixed according to the power and position of the master. A few days ago, while a portion of the street was being repaired by an European firm, a party of slaves, belonging to an influential Arab, had occasion to pass, but instead of making a detour of a short distance they broke down the temporary barricade and fought their way through. Their cry was " We are not the slaves of Europeans; we are the slaves of such a one." The Zanzibar slaves, although a miserably degraded class when brought to the island, do not afterwards occupy the lowest scale of a slave population, and they are not the enduring, isolated, beasts of burden that some suppose them to be. There is unity among the slaves of one master, unity even among gangs of labourers who habitually work together at one place, and a great deal more unity amongst those following common pursuits than would be supposed.

The statement has been several times made that the slaves look to their masters for protection, and it may be necessary to explain in what respect a person needs protection beyond that which the Government affords. It may be sufficient to state that in Zanzibar there is no Government, according to the meaning of the term in Europe, and no means of maintaining such a Government. In Zanzibar the great Arab landholders occupy much the same position as the feudal chiefs of former times, the Sultan being their acknowledged head, administering by the aid of his appointed judges the laws of the Koran. There being no written laws, the Koran is considered to contain, in epitome, all law, and in all cases, civil and criminal, it is the only ultimate authority to which the judges can refer. These chiefs exercise, either personally or through their deputies, magisterial authority over their slaves, in regard to the punishment of crime, the settling of disputes among themselves, and the obtaining of redress when injured or molested by others. In the latter class of cases it becomes a question between the Arab proprietors, and if not amicably arranged it may be referred to the Sultan, who can either decide the case or refer it to the judges. No Arab would allow another to punish one of his slaves although evidently guilty of some crime. The case must be referred to him, and the slave returned for punishment, if considered necessary.

In the town, and especially where Europeans are concerned, a slave guilty of some offence may be sent directly to the Sultan, but it is usual, if he is the slave of a respectable Arab, to send him to his master, who investigates the case, and punishes when guilt is evident. In the town many of the slaves belong to persons of very inferior degree, and if they consider that they are ill-treated by their masters they can complain to the judges. In the town of Zanzibar there are always a considerable number of native soldiers to maintain the authority of the Sultan, and keep order in the place, but in the country there are none. According to this patriarchal form of government it is necessary, not only for slaves, but for poor free men, to be under the protection of powerful chiefs, who really look after their interests. The slaves recognize this protection as of value, and free men, to secure this protection, often become voluntary slaves.

### 3. *Laws and Customs in regard to Slaves.*

A master is considered bound to support his slave under all circumstances and to protect him as one of his family, the slave, on the other hand, working as previously described.

Slave-holders are not necessarily slave-dealers or traders in the ordinary acceptation of the term, and in regard to the disposal of slaves there are recognised laws.

For an Arab who may possess an estate or farm to sell one of his purchased slaves would be considered an indication of extreme poverty, but to sell one born on the estate or in the household would be considered a disgrace. In the former case it would only occur from sheer necessity, but in the latter it would in ordinary cases indicate utter ruin. Slaves of notoriously bad character are often sold, the object of the master being to get them off the estate and out of the island, and they are often exposed for sale in the public market simply as a mode of punishment when other means have failed. To expose a slave thus for sale is the last degree of punishment. No Arab could traffic in his slaves, for to do such a thing would certainly lead to general desertion.

In the event of slaves on an estate being sold, owing
to the poverty or bankruptcy of the owner, families are
not parted except in the case of grown up young people,
and the same regulation holds good when, owing to the
death of the owner, the slaves are divided among the
heirs.

If a slave woman bears a child to her master the child
is free and legitimate, and has equal rights with the other
children, but if she has a child to another than her master,
the child is a slave and the property of her master whoever the father may be. The offspring of free women are
invariably free.

According to the laws of the Suni sect of Mahommedans, if a slave woman, of whatever race she may be,
bears a live child to her master she as well as the child is
free and cannot be again enslaved, but according to the
Ibāthi sect, the freedom of the mother does not necessarily
follow. It is usual however for those of this sect to grant
the mother her freedom on the birth of the child or to
secure her freedom on the death of the master.

It is customary for Arabs during illness and after
recovery to free some of their slaves, and few cases occur,
except in sudden death, where the harem is not freed.
Such cases do, however, occur, and the women of the
harem must be sold unless there is but one heir. Amongst
the small sect of Ibāthi it may occur, when there are many
heirs, that the mother of one or more of the heirs may be
sold. When such a thing happens the child purchases the
freedom of the mother, the amount paid being according
to circumstances. Transactions of this nature always
take place privately.

When an Arab frees a portion of his slaves the
selection is generally made from among the Wazalia.
Those only are freed whom the master supposes to be able
to understand the privileges of freedom and to provide
for themselves, the reason alleged being that were newly
imported slaves freed, their condition would not be

improved; that they would run the risk of being enslaved again or wander about living by plunder.

As previously remarked a slave may possess property and over it the master has no control whatever. There are many slaves in Zanzibar who are persons of considerable wealth and importance and the owners of other slaves; hence it is not uncommon for a slave to purchase his own liberty, although it more frequently happens that he purchases other slaves. Indeed when a slave can accumulate sufficient money he almost invariably invests it in this way. In the event of a slave having property being sold or transferred he still retains his property and the new master cannot interfere with it, he is however his slave's heir.

If a slave is dissatisfied or ill-treated he can compel his master to sell him. As a matter of fact this probably takes place only in the case of small holders, while wealthy and influential Arabs would maintain that the slaves were entirely under their own jurisdiction.

Cases of this kind are undoubtedly brought before the judges; and the judge, if the slave makes good his case, can order his sale.

A female slave is not required to work after the eighth month of pregnancy, nor during forty days after delivery.

Doubtless these and many other regulations are not quite invariably observed, especially as regards newly imported slaves, but at the same time it must be admitted that the slaves in Zanzibar, under Arab masters, have many peculiar privileges, and that the Arab is by no means a hard taskmaster.

Although the Mahommedan law, "an eye for an eye, a tooth for a tooth," does not hold good between master and slave, still, as a class, they are not exposed to wanton cruelty. Slave-owners in Zanzibar cannot believe in the accounts of the gladiatorial exhibitions of ancient Rome, where the slaves were compelled to fight in mortal combat with wild beasts, or with each other, for the amusement of a ferocious populace; and they are equally puzzled to understand how the Europeans could keep their slaves in subjection under the barbarous conditions of their bondage.

According to the accounts of writers of acknowledged veracity, the treatment of slaves by Europeans generally, and by the Anglo-Saxon race in particular, has been characterised by circumstances of extreme atrocity, the slave being regarded simply as an animal. Christians held slaves in defiance of their own religious tenets, whereas Mahommedans do so in accordance with their religious belief. This does not mitigate the *essential* evil of slavery, nor does it form any reason against the suppression of slavery; it merely indicates certain difficulties in its accomplishment.

### 4. *Condition of Freeborn and Freed Negroes.*

It will be necessary to make some remarks on the state of the free-born and freed coloured population of Zanzibar, and first on the Wahadimu.

The Wahadimu are the aboriginal inhabitants of the islands of Zanzibar, Monfia, and Pemba, as well as of many of the towns of the east coast  The reigning family is said to be of mixed Arab and Persian extraction, and the representative, Sultan Ahmed, now about seventeen years of age, maintains authority, by the permission of the Arab Sultan, over his own people.

Sultan Ahmed possesses large estates on the island, and his subjects, who are a mixed negroid race, have their villages principally on the eastern side of the island, and towards the northern and southern extremities. They occupy between sixty and seventy villages, and each village is governed by its head magistrate, or Sheha, according to their ancient manners and customs.

The native Sultan has merely a delegated power, and in all cases where the interests of Arabs are involved, judgment is given by the Zanzibar judges. The Wahadimu are free men, and they pay taxes to their own

Sultan, who can also demand their services on his estates when required. The late Seyd Majid, Sultan of Zanzibar, exacted from these people an additional capitation tax, from which he derived annually ten thousand dollars, and he also enforced their service on his estates during the clove crop season, but his brother and successor, Seyd Bargash, immediately on his succession to the government, abrogated the tax, on the ground that it was unjust and oppressive. The present Sultan has taken an interest in regard to the Wahadimu, and has compelled his Arab subjects to restore to them the lands upon which they had encroached.

The Wahadimu are a very industrious, hard-working class of people. Many of them gain their livelihood by fishing, cutting of firewood, both on the island and mainland, and some of them possess small craft, with which they bring the produce of their industry to the town from distant parts of the island. Several possess land of their own, but others have land in common, the produce of which is shared by those engaged in the cultivation.

They frequently arrange with neighbouring Arab proprietors for the cultivation of rice land, taking a certain proportion of the crop for their own share. The villages of the Wahadimu are much superior to those of the ordinary slave population, and the larger of them have a school and mosque. They are all Mahommedans, and many of them own slaves. The slaves of the Wahadimu are nearly on an equal footing with their masters, as they both engage in the same kind of work, and fare equally. Although they still maintain, under sufferance, a distinct national existence, they are gradually disappearing as a class wherever the Arab influence predominates.

The Wahadimu are quite distinct from freed slaves and the descendants of freed slaves, and they form the connecting link between the strictly Arab and negro population.

In the Island of Zanzibar there must be a large number of free and freed men of direct negro descent, far exceeding in number that of the Wahadimu population, for not only do the Arabs free many of their slaves, but, in addition, great numbers have been freed through the interposition of the British Consuls. It would be next to impossible to ascertain the ultimate destination of the slaves freed by Arabs, but thousands have been freed within the last few years, through the interposition of the British Government, the slaves having being held by Indo-British subjects, and they, being under British protection, may be accounted for. There should not be less than from four to five thousand negroes under the direct and immediate protection of the British Government in Zanzibar; but they do not appear as a distinct class amongst the negro population. It would be a matter of great interest and of paramount importance to know what has become of these freed slaves, and whether they have enjoyed and availed themselves of their privileges as British subjects. Such data would be of the greatest value as indicating what would be likely to take place in the event of the general liberation of the slave population, but unfortunately such have not been placed before the public. As a matter of fact the estates, worked by slave labour, and owned by Indo-British subjects have been disposed of to Arabs, a very few having been retained merely as places of resort on festive occasions. Amongst the negro population there is practically no distinction whatever between free and slave labour. In appearance, mode of work and living, and also in regard to pay, there is no distinction whatever, and even amongst the domestic servants of Europeans, it cannot be known, except in case of special enquiry, who are slaves and who are free. There is never any assertion made as to the condition of freedom, and it is never put forth as a plea for the employment of the individual, nor as a reason to lead one to expect that the performance of duties may be of a superior nature. This is very remarkable, as in all ages and in all countries there has been

# page

a broad line of distinction between the slaves and free, or freed men, whereas in Zanzibar there is none in regard to the negro population. The slaves on an estate may be emancipated, and in the event of such an estate being transferred to another owner, who may be legally entitled to hold slaves, the freed men generally remain if they are allowed to do so under their former privileges.

The absence of a well marked line of distinction between free men and slaves may be accounted for by the existence of the feudal system, under which all require special protection, and by the fact that recently-imported slaves recognize and act upon the right, when they can do so, of disposing of their children as slaves, even although they themselves are free.

Under the former class of cases there exists the system of voluntary slavery or servitude, and under the latter, that of the absolute disposal of children, or their disposal conditionally, the payment being redeemable.

Voluntary slavery or servitude does exist, but not under the same conditions as described by Dr. Livingstone, according to which the voluntary slave receives a money payment for himself. Free men do enroll themselves as slaves, or place themselves in the precise condition of such, that they may obtain the protection, and be under the jurisdiction of some powerful master. They may belong to any class of the slave population, and they are treated as such in every respect with this exception, that they cannot be sold by their masters.

A freed slave generally remains in the same condition as formerly, while his master is alive, and he may do so with his heirs and successors, or he may transfer himself to another master if he so chooses. This is very common amongst the free people on the coast, who are removed from the centre of Government at Zanzibar, and who wish to avail themselves of the protection of influential Arabs resident on the coast, or their deputies. When their services are required their acknowledged master has always the prior claim, and they are bound to obey his orders. It is said that many Arabs have thousands of such people under their absolute control who are directly governed by their deputies, and who do, in fact, act in accordance with the instructions of their masters.

To an ambitious Arab this is a source of great power and influence, and to the voluntary slave, or serf, it is a solid protection, the power of his master being exercised if necessary on his behalf.

In illustration of the latter class of cases, viz., the selling of children by their parents, it may be sufficient to refer to a case that very recently occurred. A number of freed slaves, under the special protection and jurisdiction of the British Consul, who are resident on an estate in the neighbourhood of Zanzibar, complained to their 'former master, that one of their number, placed in charge over them, was in the habit of selling their children and pocketing the proceeds. They did not object to the act of selling, in itself considered, but they considered themselves aggrieved at being deprived of the proceeds to which they alleged themselves entitled. They considered that they had a perfect right to dispose of their children as they themselves thought proper.

Probably in maintaining, and confessedly having acted upon this right, they merely wished to recompense themselves for the trouble and expense of bringing up their children, and not altogether from any selfish heartless disregard for the future welfare of their offspring.

These freed men had been directly imported slaves from the interior of Africa, and the children thus disposed of could not have been more than five years of age.

Probably their ideas regarding their right of selling their own children at this tender age, may have been derived from the customs of their own country, but it would be difficult to understand how such people could be dealt with according to British law, to which they were and are amenable.

## 5. *Recommendations of the Commission.*

In the Report of the Commission on the East African Slave Trade, paragraphs 61—72, contain recommendations regarding the disposal of liberated slaves, and the principal locality selected is the Island of Zanzibar.

It will be necessary, in order to test the value of these recommendations, to consider who these liberated slaves are.

With the exception of a minute fractional number, the liberated slaves are those captured by British cruizers specially employed in the suppression of the slave trade. Part of them are those captured in the legalized traffic but during an illegal time, and the remainder, forming the greatest number, are those captured from persons engaged in what may be designated the contraband trade, their destination being the various ports of Arabia. In the former class of cases the slaves are the property of subjects of the Sultan of Zanzibar, principally resident on the island, and in the latter class of cases the slaves are purchased or kidnapped by Arabs for exportation. Formerly a proclamation was issued in Zanzibar forbidding any one from selling slaves to Northern Arabs engaged in this illegal traffic, and under severe penalties no one was to afford house accommodation or even the means of sustenance to those thus engaged. The proclamation was never enforced, and remained from the first a dead letter. I am not aware that it was ever attempted to be enforced in a single instance.

In May, 1869, or thereabout, the boats of H.M.S. "Nymphe" were engaged in the capture of a slave dhow, within a few yards of the harbour of Zanzibar. One of the crew was killed, and an officer wounded. The Arabs engaged in the fight, whose tribe and place of residence in the town were perfectly well known, were allowed to walk about for more than a month, and to leave the island without any punishment having been inflicted, in so far as was known to those who took an interest in the

matter. The Arabs referred to had only one dhow, and
they did not number more than ten men. This having
occurred in the time of H. H. Seyd Majid, late Sultan of
Zanzibar, does not impress one with the value of proclamations, nor with the actual power of H.M. Consul in
redressing injuries inflicted on those actually engaged in
Her Majesty's service.

The captured slaves, who are recommended to be
placed in the island of Zanzibar, may thus be divided
into three classes. First, those who previous to capture
were owned by individuals resident in Zanzibar, or in the
neighbouring coast towns; second, those kidnapped by
northern Arabs, formerly owned by the same class of
people; and third, those purchased by northern Arabs,
and shipped north in a contraband manner. A fourth
class might be added, viz., those sent on speculation by
companies in Zanzibar, who jointly engage in a venture
of ten or more slaves each. Those purchased by northern
Arabs, on their own account, form but a very small proportion of those actually shipped to the north, so that
the Commission recommend that the captured slaves
should be landed as free men at the very doors of their
former owners. In one point of view in which the
liberated slaves may be regarded simply as Africans, the
proposition is not unreasonable, as they are placed in their
own country, but when the ultimate views, as expressed
by the Commission, are taken into account, it does seem
extraordinary that such a course should have been dreamt
of. In paragraph 65, it is stated as follows:—" We have
" been induced to select this place, not only from its central
" position in the midst of the slave-trading districts, and
" the facilities which it therefore affords for the slaves being
" speedily landed from the cruizers ; but because we under-
" stand that there is a great and increasing demand for free
" labour at that place, and that even children can readily
" obtain work at good wages, so that no charge for their
" maintenance is likely to be thrown on the Imperial

" Government." Various suggestions are thereafter made, scarcely worthy of serious consideration, according to which the freed slave is to be efficiently protected by Her Majesty's Consul, although amenable to the laws of Zanzibar.

Every caravan or trading expedition that leaves Zanzibar, or the mainland for the interior, is to a greater or less extent engaged in the slave trade, and they return to the coast at all seasons of the year with ivory and slaves. For eight months in the year slaves can be conveyed, according to treaty with Great Britain, to and from certain places within the Sultan's dominions, but during the months of January, February, March, and April such traffic is not allowed, and all captures are legal. If a caravan arrives, say in the month of January, at the coast with slaves, a slave-owner may run the risk of shipping them to Zanzibar rather than incur the expense of maintaining them on the coast for three months. If these slaves are captured and landed as freed men at Zanzibar, can it be supposed that the slave-dealer will cease to regard them as his property, and abstain from all efforts to get possession of them, and afterwards dispose of them? If a party of so-called northern Arabs kidnap a number of slaves belonging to Zanzibar men, and if these slaves are captured by British cruizers and returned to the doors of their former owners, can any one imagine that these freed men or children are safe, even although under the special protection of Her Majesty's Consul? To propose such a course seems to be merely trifling with the most important interests of our fellow-beings.

The slaves landed differ greatly in point of intelligence, but many appear to be utter savages, and are in a state of complete nudity, or with a band of twisted leaves round their loins. They are strangers and entirely ignorant of the language of Zanzibar, and often are in a shocking state of emaciation. The Commission recommend, in order to their personal safety, that they should have " printed certificates of freedom," that " a

" register should be kept of them at the British Consulate," and that " the first object of the Consul should be to obtain " employment for them as free labourers in Zanzibar." It is also stated that there being a great demand for free labour "no charge for their maintenance is likely to be thrown " upon the Imperial Government."

A greater amount of absurdity could not be compressed into less space. Slavery is to be effectually, through gradually, suppressed, by the introduction of this class of free labour. Everything is supposed to work smoothly and cost nothing to the Imperial Government. Her Majesty's Consul is to obtain employment for them, and no one is supposed to kidnap or molest them, because their names are registered, and they have printed certificates of freedom. What Consul will undertake to carry out his proposed duties? Who will undertake to spell the names of these wretched people? Where are they to carry their printed certificates of freedom?

But supposing that these difficulties regarding their freedom are successfully got over, one is quite entitled to enquire where and how is Her Majesty's Consul to obtain employment for them as free labourers?

There is nothing in the past to induce one to place any confidence in these specious proposals. In the absence of all information on the subject it may be fairly asked, what has become of all those slaves liberated by the influence of Her Majesty's Consuls in Zanzibar? The question may be limited to within the last five years, or the last five months. What account can be given of them? Are they dead or alive? Are they free, or in the condition of slaves, or have they been kidnapped? I venture to state that neither Her Majesty's Consul, nor Her Majesty's Acting-Consul, know anything at all about them, except in so far as information has been conveyed in the ordinary course of friendly meetings. During the last five years I have never heard of any Consul making any enquiries regarding the Negro-British subjects in

Zanzibar, and no such enquiries could have been made officially without my knowledge.

In regard to the value and importance of Consular supervision and protection certain cases may be quoted.

In paragraph 9 of the Commission's Report, it is stated that the Galla tribes, in the neighbourhood of Fazi, had been incited to go to war by the slave-dealers in order to procure slaves. Without assenting to the accuracy of this statement it may be sufficient to admit that some of the Galla captives, who were enslaved, were captured by the "Daphne" and "Star," and brought to Zanzibar. Two of these freed Galla slaves were received into the house of Her Majesty's Consul, and one into the house of Her Majesty's Vice-Consul. Of the former, one a female, died, and the other, on the departure of Her Majesty's Consul from Zanzibar, was left without any arrangements for his support or disposal. On the representations of Her Majesty's Acting-Consul the boy was received into the establishment of the Universities Mission, where he is now. The one taken charge of by Her Majesty's Vice-Consul became lazy and insolent, declined to obey reasonable orders, and left. He now gains his livelihood in a very disreputable manner. If such is the result regarding liberated slaves in the Consulate, what can be expected throughout the island generally?

The members of the Commission do not, in their Report, condescend to give any explanation as to how or where Her Majesty's Consul is to obtain employment for the freed slaves, as free labourers in Zanzibar, but the facility for doing so may have been understood without any necessity for entering into details.

Difficulties, however, do crop up in considering the feasibility of the scheme. The largest employers of labour are the Arab landowners whose estates are worked by slaves, or by free men whose relations to the proprietor are precisely the same as those of slaves.

I believe that no Arab would receive on his estate

newly imported Africans on whom legal rights had been conferred of a much higher class than what he himself possessed. Arabs might do so under the conviction that the arrangement was a mere matter of talk between the Consul and himself, and that the negro, utterly ignorant of his high status, would be to all intents and purposes his slave. I have inquired of some of the most respectable Arab landowners if they would receive on their estates such people, who had the power of lodging complaints against them, or their deputies, at the British Consulate, and the invariable answer has been "No." It must be taken for granted that if the rights of free men are to be conferred on liberated slaves, and that if these rights are to be of any value, they must be not only explained to them, but properly understood, else the conferring of freedom is merely a mockery.

In the event of one of these people being kidnapped he would find that his printed certificate of freedom would not act like a charm when presented to his captor.

But it may not have been contemplated to place these liberated slaves on the estates, as thousands of people are daily employed in town, and can always obtain labour if competent.

Probably the Indo-British subjects might take a considerable number as domestic servants, as they would save about half a dollar per month on each, but if they were required to pay on the same terms as for slaves, they would continue their present arrangements, as they can return the slaves to their masters in case of dissatisfaction or illness. These people have already had the experience of liberated slaves on their estates, and they would not be likely to repeat the experiment except under very different circumstances.

The European and American firms, and also many natives, are large employers of daily labourers. They might be induced to employ free labourers in preference to slaves, provided that the quality of work was the same but I feel assured that not one would take over a lot of these people, undertaking to support and protect them as the masters of slaves do, in return for the work done, the freed slaves being under the special protection of Her Majesty's Consul. This has been already fairly tried in Zanzibar, and out of sixty freed slaves, only one remains in the same employment. Where they have been dispersed no one knows, but some have been enslaved. Since the Report of the Commission has been made public in Zanzibar, freed slaves have been landed on the island, and some have been transferred to the mainland.

Dr. Kirk, Her Majesty's Acting-Consul and Political Agent, has informed me and other British residents here, that to some of these freed slaves, whose work was not satisfactory to those to whom they had been handed over by him, he had given certificates of freedom, authorizing the parties to whom they had been entrusted to turn them adrift. To prevent any misconception, I may state that those to whom these freed slaves were given in charge were the priests of the Roman Catholic Mission in Zanzibar who possess an estate on the mainland at Bagamoyo. The system of disposal at the present date, June, 1871, is as follows. A liberated slave, a free man, and a protected subject, is handed over, without consulting his own wishes, say to the Roman Catholic Priests. This liberated slave who, is under the special protection of Her Majesty's Consul, and who probably is an utter savage, does not work satisfactorily to these men, and they represent the case to the Consul, who writes out a certificate of freedom and turns him adrift.

Such cases have occurred, not in remote times, but within the last few months.

In regard to these liberated slaves the Commission states " that no charge for their maintenance is likely to " be thrown upon the Imperial Government," and this is evidently a strong point. Expense, however, will fall upon some parties, or else many of the freed slaves will die of utter starvation and neglect.

A few years ago, out of about seven hundred freed

slaves, recently brought from the mainland, one hundred and forty-three were on my hospital list. These were all severe cases, and trifling ailments were not taken into account. Every means available were placed at my disposal for the treatment of these cases, and no expense was spared to promote the recovery of these people. They suffered from dysentery, syphilis, primary, secondary, and tertiary; malignant ulcerations of the most severe form, generally ending in death or necessitating amputation; and paludal fever in its various forms. During the whole of my experience as a medical man, as house surgeon in a large general hospital and in visiting hospitals in Great Britain and the Continent, I have never seen such revolting cases of disease.

Even to a medical man, who had gone through the routine of the dissecting-room, and as dresser in the surgical wards of an hospital, such sights were sickening. Three days ago one of the liberated slaves landed from H.M.S. "Dryad," was placed under my professional care suffering from a sloughing ulcer over the head of the femur, and nearly exposing the bone, and yet in apparently utter ignorance of the subject on which they report, the Commission say in regard to these people " that no " charge for their maintenance is likely to be thrown upon " the Imperial Government."

A more reckless statement was never penned. One would naturally suppose that, on the liberated slaves being brought to the Consulate, the whole affair would be settled by Her Majesty's Consul saying, Well, my good friends, you can get employment to-morrow morning if you appear at half-past five at any of the European houses, and you can get furnished lodgings at the houses of such a one or such a one. I will register your name at the Consulate, and here are your printed certificates of freedom. If any one ill-treats or molests you, come to me, and don't forget to do so if you are kidnapped by the northern Arabs. You are amenable to the laws of Zanzibar, but under the special protection of me, Her Majesty's Consul. The liberated slaves shoulder their bundles and proceed to make their domestic arrangements. And so the great problem as regarding slavery is settled!

### 6. *Slave Trade in the Interior and its Cure.*

Paragraphs 4—7 of the Report treat on this subject, and the supposed mode in which this traffic is carried on in the interior of Africa is very forcibly described, although in all probability the description is that of very rare and exceptional cases, as it does not correspond with what the slaves themselves state. It is said that the " slave-dealers " start for the interior well armed and provided with " articles for the barter of slaves, such as beads and cotton " cloth," and that, " on arriving at the scene of their " operations they incite and sometimes help the natives of " one tribe to make war upon another." It is perfectly correct that slave-dealers start for the interior well armed, and it is equally correct that armed parties start every morning and evening from the various districts of Zanzibar to pay their respects to His Highness the Sultan, and that armed Arabs with their armed retinues call upon the writer daily for medical advice. The arms of an Arab are as essential articles of dress as his turban, and no expedition, whatever its nature may be, ever starts from Zanzibar without being armed. The description of the mode of operation in the procuring of slaves by the Arabs is denied by those engaged in the traffic, and is not corroborated by the statements of the slaves themselves. No higher authority, for what he has actually witnessed, can be quoted than Dr. Livingstone, who in various parts of his work on "The Zambezi and its Tributaries," describes what he actually saw, but on a careful perusal of such portions, there does not appear to be any reason for the statements made by the Commission regarding the operations of Zanzibar Arabs.

In 1868 Dr. Livingstone writes from Central Africa

regarding a party of Arabs whom he there met, and states that they supplied him with provisions, cloth, and beads. He writes, "They showed the greatest kindness and " anxiety for my safety and success." " I was glad to see " the mode of ivory and slave-trading of these men, it " formed such a perfect contrast to that of the ruffians " from Kilwa, and to the ways of the atrocious Portuguese " from Tette, who were connived at in their murders by " the Governor D'Almeida."

Dr. Livingstone and Captains Burton, Speke, and Grant do not exactly coincide in their statements regarding the Slave Trade in the interior, and it is not surprising that this should be the case, for they have. severally seen it under different aspects, modified by locality, time, and circumstances.

The paragraphs on the Slave Trade in the interior cannot be received as anything like an accurate generalization of what has been published on the subject, far less of what can be obtained in Zanzibar, with very little trouble, by interrogating the slaves themselves, and they may be described as the sensational part of the Report. The principal trading expeditions start from the mainland between Kilwa to the south, and the Pangani to the north, and every one is, to a greater or less extent, connected with the Slave Trade. In regard to organization they are much the same, the goods for barter varying according to the different localities for which they are bound. They traverse the whole country to beyond the Lake Regions, and from the Portuguese settlements to the south, to beyond the Equator on the north. In all these extensive regions they trade with the most savage tribes, the Maviti to the west of Nyassa, and the Masai to the north-west of the Kilimanjaro and Kinya mountains. These expeditions may be absent from one to three years, while others doing business with the more maritime tribes may be absent from two to three or four months. They take with them principally the mercantile products of

Europe, America, and India, the larger caravans bring back ivory and slaves, and the smaller ivory, slaves, cattle, and a variety of articles. The principal returns from the Kilwa caravans are slaves and a little ivory; those from the Bagamoyo caravans, passing to the Nyamwezi country, and from thence branching out in all directions; and from the Pangani caravans, which traverse the regions of the Masai, are ivory and a few slaves.

These expeditions are not predatory but mercantile. They are all armed and fully prepared to act on the defensive, if necessary. Some of them consist of two thousand men on starting from the coast, the greater number of whom are slaves. The people whom they visit require cloth and ornaments of various kinds, such as beads and brass wire, and the only articles that they can give in return are ivory and slaves, and near the coast, oxen and goats. In order to procure these articles they hunt the elephant, pick up the tusks of dead animals, capture the people of neighbouring tribes for sale as slaves, and sell their own children and younger brothers and sisters, and those engaged in the expedition do not hesitate to pick up and kidnap any stragglers from the villages whom they can seize. If these people had other articles that they could give in exchange they would probably cease to traffic in their own race, but they have not, and until some means are afforded for opening up Africa by means of roads, whereby the resources of the country can be developed and conveyed to the coast, the slave trade must continue. If the means of transit in certain directions were afforded, the resources of the country would be gradually developed, and slavery would die a natural death.

His Highness Seyd Bargash, the present Sultan, proposes to open up a road as far as Khutu, on the great ivory caravan route towards the Nyamwezi country, but it will be difficult for him to to do so with his slender revenue. This road would, in itself, eventually pay, and would tend in no small degree to open up a large district.

Until such means of communication are opened up, Africa must remain as it at present is: and were slavery abolished at its very origin, the natives would simply be necessitated to do without a proportion of their cloth and ornaments, there being nothing but ivory to give in return.

The natives in the interior traffic in slaves because they have nothing else that they can traffic with. If they possessed cattle or vegetable products, which they could barter for cloth and beads, they would cease to traffic in their own kind, for parents would come to see that their children were a source of wealth.

The means uselessly expended by the British Government annually in the suppression of the slave trade, would go far to meet the requirements of the case, slavery would receive its death-blow, and a new market would be opened up to the civilized world of unlimited extent.

If the Commission had recommended the establishment of an East African Liberia, and if instead of saying " that " no expense is likely to be entailed on the Imperial Govern- " ment," they had stated quite the contrary, viz., that no scheme worth the paper on which it was written could be proposed without expense being entailed on the Imperial Government, they would have spoken much more sensibly.

One or more of the small islands fringing the African coast might be available as the beginning of such a scheme, or a tract of country on the mainland might be obtained for the disposal of the freed slaves. Then their liberty would be a boon, not a mere name, a caricature on liberty. A nucleus would be gradually formed which would here-after exert an immense influence on this side of the continent; and this, combined with reasonable means for opening up the country by roads, beginning with the caravan lines, on which roads would pay, would gradually extinguish slavery in all its forms, simply because the traffic in human beings would cease to be profitable to either seller or buyer.

JAMES CHRISTIE, M.A., M.D.

www.ingramcontent.com/pod-product-compliance
Lightning Source LLC
Chambersburg PA
CBHW022025080426
42733CB00007B/723